The Black Youth Manual

Black Boys Guide to Triumphing Through Adversity

Emanuel Grimes

First Edition

ISBN: 979-8647542038

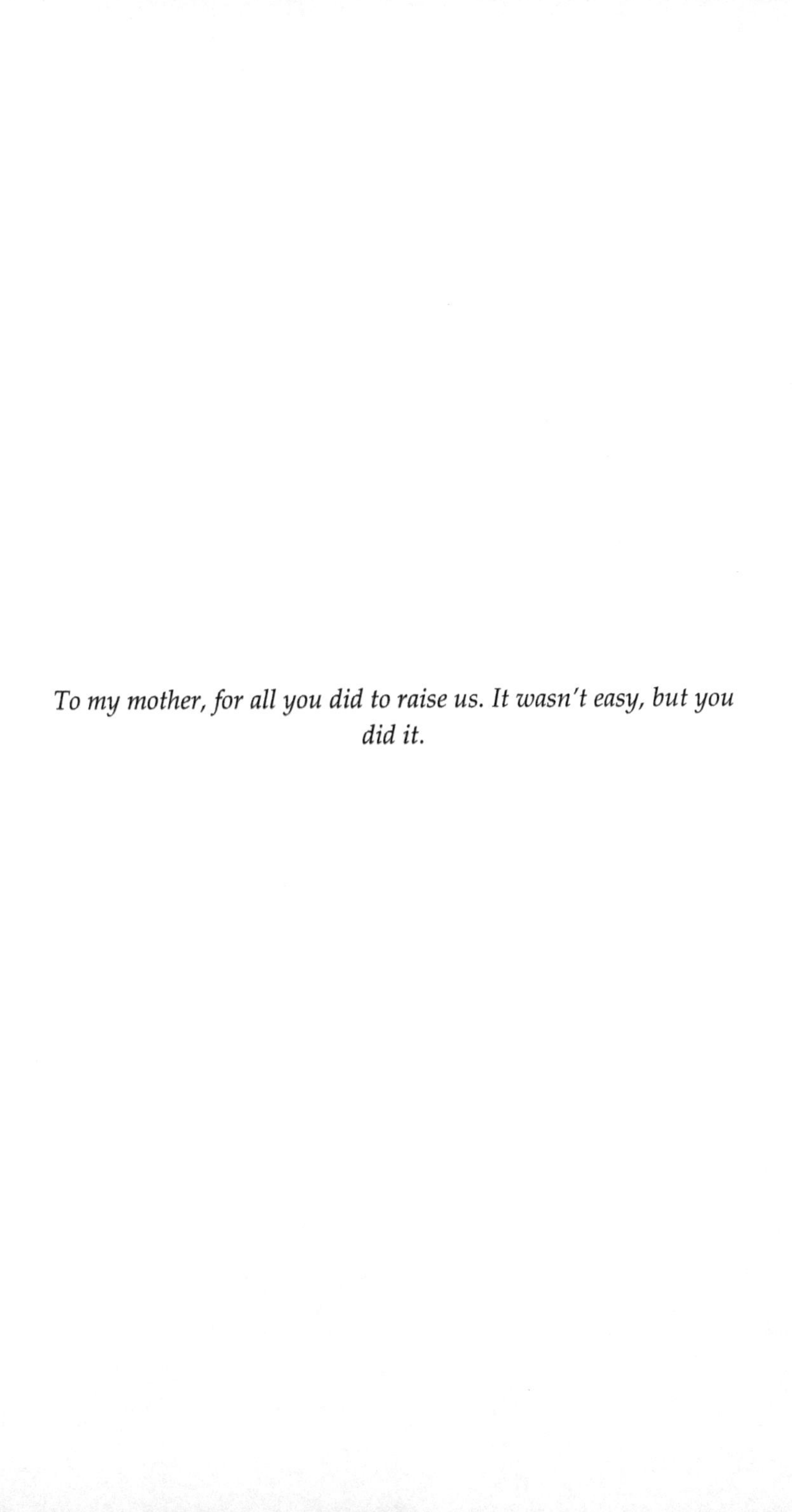

To my mother, for all you did to raise us. It wasn't easy, but you did it.

Contents

Introduction 1

Chapter 1 ‖ Who's poor? Not me…right? 11

Neighbor "hood" 13

Gang Culture 16

Education 20

Foods You Consume...22

Mentality 25

Chapter 2 ‖ Ok, What About the Police?....................31

"I don't like the police"...31

How the police think 33

How to survive 34

Chapter 3 ‖ Social Media: A Two-Way Sword...............39

Perception vs. Reality 40

Social media is the best invention ever 41

I hate social media 42

Chapter 4 ‖ Education 45

The basics: Graduating high school 46

The college experience 47

Chapter 5 ‖ Church..51

Church as crutch 53

A challenge to outdated principles..........................55

Chapter 6 ‖ Five Life Tips to Follow as a Man 59

Finances and spending 59

Appearance 61

Doctor 62

Relationships with women 62

Father your children 63

Company you keep 63

Chapter 7 ‖ Tips for Educators and Parents....................65

Chapter 8 ‖ Notable Leaders in Our Community 69

Lebron James 69

Nipsey Hussle 70

Colin Kaepernick 73

Introduction

Back in college, I received a book called *A Framework for Understanding Poverty* by Ruby K. Payne. In this book, she analyzes the distinct differences between social classes, with a focus on those living in poverty. At first, I thought it was just another book. But as she went into detail describing the hidden rules of each class, I was forced to rethink everything I had come to know. She explained that the poor, middle, and wealthy each have expectations of what they should do or know as a part of said class. Everyone in their respective classes knows what is expected of them and they live by certain rules. I came to understand that the mannerisms and beliefs deemed normal in my upbringing were merely a part of the social class I was associated with. How I viewed the world was formulated and influenced by my family's socioeconomic status. I grew up in poverty by all definitions of the word, so it was interesting reading what she had to say about that structure.

Reflecting back on my childhood I can clearly see mistakes that were made, especially regarding finances. It is very common for individuals living in poverty to feel like no matter what type of compensation they receive, it will first be spent on wants and needs secondary. There is no thought or consideration about the future, only what the money can get them now. When you are poor, money is scarce, so when you do get it, you just spend it. Even though bills are due, it feels good to look nice and gain a temporary boost of confidence. It's the simple things that matter to those living in poverty because at least, for the moment, it helps them alleviate the overwhelming burdens they face on the daily.

In the past and even presently, I know, and have witnessed impoverished families in urban communities receive thousands of dollars back from their income tax returns every year. Sadly, they can't tell you what they did with it. Nothing of importance to help their unfavorable situations can be accounted for, such as paying off credit cards and past due bills, making car repairs, or placing money in a savings account. The logic behind not handling these important financial responsibilities is that bills will always be there. Even if you pay them they will keep coming, so you might as well buy something you want.

What people are experiencing in my opinion is a conditioned sense of helplessness. For the longest time, I thought the same way. After all, it seems right. So how do you fix this? Some would assume that the problem could be fixed if people living with insufficient resources were given a livable wage. This would help out initially. But because these individuals lack financial literacy, there is a tendency to misuse funds. Money management and saving isn't taught to people living in poverty; it just isn't useful. People are living check to check, so there is never any money available to consider saving.

To illustrate how this applies, think about some young black men from poverty-stricken communities who managed, through hard work and drive, to become professional athletes. A lot of these guys would go broke after retiring—and some even during their playing careers—because they did a horrible job of managing their funds. Many of these athletes grew up without means and now that they do doesn't make them financial literate all of a sudden. They make the same poor monetary decisions as their peers in the neighborhoods they are from. They would spend lump sums of money and recklessly buy everything their eyes would see because they believed they may never have that money again. Sure, they were making more than enough money to survive and have the finer things, but they lacked the discipline and knowledge to properly allocate their funds. Because this was happening so frequently to young black athletes, the NBA incorporated a money management workshop for all rookies, to give them the skills needed to make sound financial decisions

* * *

So, in relation to finances, growing up in poverty negatively affects your decision making as an adult. But how much of an effect does living in poverty have on your behavior? If you do rise out, will those behaviors stay with you? These are questions that have to be answered. When I look at my own actions,

I admit that there have been times I wanted to act out when confronted with certain issues. I'm sure if everybody could do and say what they wanted to people they would. But you learn that your actions can affect others, their perspective of you, and how they treat you. Due to learning to control my actions and behaviors, making smarter decisions became easier. Is that enough to deter someone who grew up in a hostile environment and has learned to exercise discipline to actually exercise it?

I decided to test my hypothesis out on other famous public figures who frequently talk about being raised in impoverished communities. Observing their behavior it is very noticeable their upbringing still had an effect on their morals, beliefs, and character. For instance, I have seen numerous people of color, who grew up poor and happen to become successful, commit crimes. This caused me to ask myself, "Why do people who have money still make horrible decisions?" I am specifically addressing rappers whose main identity is to rap about life, the struggle, and how they made it out. Although their stories are captivating and the main reason they rose to stardom, what they fail to realize is that the effects of growing up in poverty is still something they haven't dealt with, and until they do it will forever be a part of them.

Famous rappers such as T.I., Lil Wayne, and Kodak Black have earned millions of dollars from their craft, yet they have been arrested for possessing firearms because they are convicted felons. Well why would they carry guns if they have security or hired police to protect them? It may very well be that no matter how much security they have, they still don't feel safe. They could be so used to watching their own back and protecting themselves that they feel they are the only person who can protect them. Sounds crazy, but it's actually pretty normal. If that's the environment you come from it's going to take time and effort to ease away from that way of thinking. This is no excuse to justify their actions, but to put in perspective some issues they may be dealing with. Gaining access to money catapulted them out of their hostile environments, but couldn't erase a lifestyle that has been ingrained into their being.

There is no quick fix for living in poverty. There are too many variables to address that all have to work together to get individuals and families to start the process. Understanding its impact on one's mental, emotional, and financial growth requires relearning everything they were ever taught. Poverty is like a cancer. It can spread to other parts of the body if left untreated. So when people don't have resources it stunts their growth in every area of their lives, from access to quality health care and education, to food choices and housing options

* * *

The effects of living in poverty and its components can be for life. You have to relearn everything you have ever known, or been taught, to change your mindset. *A Framework for Understanding Poverty* enlightened me on how it affects every part of a child's life, which can carry even into adulthood. This is why you have to address it during childhood. I have lived it, and I have learned to overcome it.

I want to share with you what I have seen and endured growing up in unfavorable environments and how you can rise above it. Here, you will learn how poverty affects the mentality, behaviors, and outlook on life of young black males, like you. One of the main reasons I'm writing this book is to relate with you, and other young men like you, about your experiences. I want you to know that you are not alone.

A little bit about me

My situation was not the best, but I wasn't mad at anyone. I grew up in a single-parent home with my five siblings. We had the same struggles as any other family living in the inner city. We didn't have much money, reliable transportation, or many resources. But there was something about our family that didn't let our unfortunate situation define us. In fact, I took an interest in it. I started questioning the world around me. Observing the interactions of adults with other adults, adults with kids, and adults with authority figures fascinated me. Naturally, I'm a calm and relaxed person, so I tried to apply logic to everything. Confrontations were my specialty or let's just say what I was most intrigued by. What I noticed when it came to confrontations was that most people acted out of pure emotion. There was no space to apply logic because logic required you to think, and thinking was frowned upon. Thinking required you to come up with a plausible solution, but that didn't matter because the other party probably wasn't into that. Problem solving is shunned upon but violence and chaos is welcome. It was unbelievable. You are expected to just react and say eff the consequences because, no matter what, you had to prove your dominance. You had to get your street cred.

People lived by standards deemed acceptable to their community, not by the world in general. People had their own morals, values, and beliefs that they stood by without consideration of ethics, laws, or consequences. For example, it was common knowledge or "code" that if someone was to physically hurt or kill one of your home boys, you were supposed to go get revenge. You couldn't just tell the police, or you would be considered a snitch, therefore making you a target of retaliation. You also couldn't refuse to ride on the guys that shot your friend because they would say you are soft or you wasn't real. Then, they would basically disassociate with you.

Dissociation has consequences. It would mean that you had not only lost the trust of your gang— your peers—but that they may impose harm on you. These are crazy situations one had to deal with and at that time I came to see as acceptable behavior. Once my eyes were opened I realized that that lifestyle was a maze. People were just walking around with no direction, no moral code, and no goals. I said to myself, "Until these people are removed from their environment to see a different way to live, they won't see the destruction they are causing." I knew this to be true, because I was taken out the same environment eight hours a day to attend school in the suburbs.

I attended inner-city schools all the way up until the sixth grade. Then, I became part of the Voluntary Interdistrict Choice Corporation (VICC) program. This program facilitated transfers of city students to suburban school districts and suburban students to city magnet schools. African American students living in the city could commute to the suburbs for school and non-African American students from the suburbs could attend magnet schools in St. Louis City. VICC was established to increase racial integration in the metropolitan area public schools. Being a part of this program allowed me to experience people living different lives and abiding by different norms than I was used to. I witnessed adults talking things out instead of arguing and saw kids taking their education seriously. And for the first time, I felt safe at school.

With that new experience, I felt I had been lied to. Coming home to complete chaos in the community around me was unsettling. It was then that I realized that the people in my neighborhood didn't have to live like this. They just didn't know any better. "If these people knew better, then they would do better" I thought.

When I began writing this book, helping young black men have a better chance at surviving and defeating odds is what I had in mind. Media continues to portray us as defiant, criminal, and impulsive. While this could be true in certain cases, it is a stereotype that some Americans, and particularly other races, seem to buy into. I have personally experienced people walking around the store watching me shop, to police asking me why I'm walking in a certain neighborhood. Young black men face all types of unfair treatment every single day of our lives. No wonder so many of us walk around with a chip on our shoulder.

In America, one's socioeconomic status, or their social class dictates the way they respond to various situations, which could mean life or death. My theory about why some black men, specifically uneducated black men, seem to have mostly negative interactions with the police is this: The lack of teaching in being civil. People in poverty-stricken neighborhood's from my experience don't usually argue civilly. People don't stop talking long enough to hear each other's point of view. It doesn't matter who is right or wrong; the only result is to fight or walk away to dissolve disputes. A lot of black males from these neighborhoods interact with police the same way. They don't respect authority and think they can argue their point until they win. In more affluent neighborhoods blacks may get harassed but not to the extent as those living in impoverished communities. Some police officers think they can harass these individuals more because the area is already crime ridden, they have no money, and no power. They don't have a voice and chances are they already have a criminal record, so that's probable cause for any stop or harassment. So when you get pulled over your first reaction might be rage and frustration, but that has to subside common sense. You may be innocent but don't feed the narrative they want you to. Elements of your livelihood and surroundings effect everything about one's existence. Sometimes, that leads to negative outcomes if not corrected.

While growing up in what most would label unsatisfactory conditions, I was blessed with the opportunity for some helpful, caring, and motivating people to step up and show me a different reality and a way of being. They showed me that my living situation did not have to define me, nor did it have to be permanent. I gained so much insight from reading *A Framework for Understanding Poverty* that I decided to return the favor to my young black brothers by writing this book. I want to show you that regardless of your situation, *you have a choice*. You have a choice to be a product of your environment or to defeat your environment. In order to defeat it, you have to get a basis of how your opinions and views of the world are formed. This starts with breaking down the most important components of your life that assist in shaping it.

Chapter 1 ‖ Who's poor? Not me…right?

What is poverty? As a young black male, you may have heard this word before. Or, you may have heard other teens closely associated with it such as poor, disadvantaged, or underserved. I wouldn't exactly expect you to know what this all means, but it is important for you to begin processing how poverty affects you and your quality of life. It doesn't matter what term is used to describe the condition of not having, you are well aware of how it feels to be in that position. Let me explain. Poverty, as defined in Merriam-Webster dictionary, is "The state of one who lacks a usual or socially acceptable amount of money or material possessions." Does this sound familiar?

Have you ever needed things but didn't have enough money to get them? I mean things as simple as toothpaste, toothbrushes, and deodorant? Have you ever needed your clothes washed but didn't have a washing machine or money to go to the laundromat, so you just hope they didn't smell and wore them again? Have you ever been hungry and repeatedly walked back and forth to the refrigerator hoping there's going to be something in there to eat this time? Have your parents ever been late on the rent for months and your family was forced to leave your residence? These are things that may seem like the norm to you. Everyone around you may even be experiencing them. But in reality, it's an unfortunate situation. Living in poverty can affect every part of your life. I mean everything—from the way you eat and think, to the way you feel and perceive life. Living in poverty takes a toll on your physical, mental, and emotional health. As a young man, it will no doubt influence your choices and your outlook on life.

If you have endured any of the occurrences I listed, chances are, you are living in poverty. You are dissatisfied with the conditions you are living in, and your parents are, as well. It is not that they don't want and aren't trying to do better for you. They just haven't been afforded the means to do so. With the limited amount of resources your parents have obtained, they are probably doing their best to stay afloat. Many times, your household is faced with choices, such as whether you are going to keep the lights on or eat. Sometimes both can't be done. Unexpected expenses come out of nowhere with no additional money saved up to cover them. Medical emergencies happen all the time, but because of a lack of insurance, there is a tendency to avoid the hospital. One problem after another seems to happen with no light in sight. You see your mom trying. But no matter what she does, it's just not enough. You see the disappointment in her eyes when she can't pay this bill or take care of that expense. You know when your parents are hurting, because you feel the hurt as well. A lot of hard decisions have to be made because of a lack of money in the household. If you regularly face any of these situations in your life currently, more than likely, you are living in poverty.

It's not about the situation but how you handle the situation. In other words, it's not what happens to you, but how you react to what happens to you that matters. You can't help that you were born into poverty. However, you can make a decision that influences whether you want to stay there or not.

The first thing you have to do is to acknowledge your situation. Recognize that you weren't dealt a fair hand in life. You can't mope around forever, though. If you do, you will become content living as you are. Second thing, say to yourself, "I am going to do something about it. I will not be a victim of my circumstances." If you can do this, you are well on your way. Promise yourself that you will do whatever it takes to not have to live in poverty as an adult. Your parents may have done all they could to provide for you, but you have to push yourself to want better. You don't have to feel guilty for this. It's okay to want more out of life. Part of the poverty mindset is settling for what you have and thinking you can't get better. These are my exact thoughts that kept me inspired to do better. And I did do better, so now I'm sharing them with you.

Neighbor "hood"

Man, oh man. Where do I start?

Fellas, let me tell you something. I know you may be proud of your 'hood. And I get it. That's where you are from, and it's all love there. Everybody knows everybody's mother, and they will feed you, your friends, and the neighborhood. You get to stay out late at night, because your mom works late, and there is no one to supervise you. These are some simple joys you get accustomed to as a youth, not really realizing that if your mom could have someone watch you, just to make sure you're safe, she would. In some cases, it's even illegal for you to be at home alone under a certain age. I know, because my mom worked overnights at one point in time, and we stayed out later than we should have sometimes.

* * *

But if we talk about the somewhat fun things, we have to introduce the negative as well. And truthfully, the bad outweighs the good. Growing up in a disadvantaged neighborhood, you have probably witnessed a lot of crime, gang violence, and unfavorable living conditions. You might reside in a single-parent household, most likely with your mother, in a neighborhood labeled as "unsafe" to live in. You may be living in a two-bedroom apartment, which is all your parents can afford. Or, you might be living in government housing. You may have three to four siblings, so multiple people have to share a bedroom. On top of that, there's never enough food to feed everyone. Sometimes, your mother can't afford to pay the electric bill and put food on the table. That means she has to choose what is more important. The truth is they are both important, so it's a lose-lose situation. You have to be able to eat, and you definitely need utilities to stay clean and be able to cook food. Now, that's just the difficulties around the household. Mom may have a car to get to work, but if the car breaks down, there is no money saved up to get it fixed quickly. This, in turn, could jeopardize her getting work every day. That could lead to her getting fired, which leads to her being late on rent and so on. The cycle never ends.

All this trauma in the home will stress you out and spill over to your schooling and behavior. You're so used to things going wrong that whenever something else goes bad you're like, "Whatever." You're just so used to being disappointed and things not working out for you. You don't want to do work at school, because you aren't motivated. You see no point in going to school, but you know you have to, so you act out when there. Teachers want you to take education seriously, but you can't see how it's going to help your current circumstances. How is reading going to fill your empty tummy right now? How is social studies going stop your family from getting evicted on Friday? These are some of the very reasons why young black men living in poverty don't value education and refuse to put much effort into it. But here's a secret that will change your life: Getting an education is the fastest and most to fix your situation long term. efficient way

With all the negatives and stressors I pointed out, there is still camaraderie amongst most individuals. The fact that we don't have everything but we're in this together. It's similar to what people where feeling around the world during the Covid 19 crisis when you were confined to your homes. When you look next door and see others going through the same struggle as you, you feel good. It's weird but it's comforting, because you don't feel alone. You have a community that doesn't have much, but at least you have each other. I know this feeling because I have lived and witnessed it. You don't need much, just good people around and you'll get through the day. Everything feels okay.

Gang Culture

As a black male, I know that gang culture is a huge problem in the African American community. Being a young black man that has lived in socioeconomically challenged neighborhoods my whole life, you can't avoid gang violence. Whether you want to believe it or not, nothing you are going through is new. Young black men before me dealt with the same issues growing up. The thing that's unavoidable about gangs is that you have to be associated with someone or some gang. Or, gangs will take you as weak and try to extort you. Most young people don't join gangs for fun; they do it for protection. If you are associated with a certain group, people won't try to fight you or will think twice because your fellow gang members might be around.

When you are in a gang, you feel empowered and safe. Yet, at the same time, you feel paranoid, because rival gangs are always looking for you. It's a path to destruction that leaves you with two options: I get them, or they get me. Many guys are pressured into the gang culture who actually want no parts of it. You are damned if you do join and damned if you don't. It's so unfair. It's very stressful. You didn't ask for this. You were thrown into it. You may lose friends and family members to senseless gun violence, and it hurts. There are also those who choose on their own to join gangs and terrorize people. Hurt people hurt people. Sometimes innocent people. For the young men caught up in the street life, let me give you this word of advice. Oftentimes, the battle you're fighting is all over an address or a street that will be there long after everyone you know is dead and gone. So, who really won? The actual street did.. the pavement, concrete, and apartments.. because they are what's left. Put that way, it makes me sick to my stomach. All the killings over nothing, when each side could have talked it out. The true struggle is that nobody feels safe, so they get mad and take it out on each other. This is what happens in the community. And then, you have to go to school where the threat can be even worse. Going to school actually puts you in direct contact with the gang members you are trying to avoid.

This was my experience with gangs growing up in the 1990s and early 2000s. Back then, gangs were more aggressive in their pursuit of members than they are today. It seems these days, they don't seek you out. You have a choice whether you want to join. They aren't just broken up in different groups like Crips and Bloods anymore. Now, they have so many branches and individuality to them. Five guys can come together now and give themselves a name and call it a gang. Gangs are more about expression, these days, but can still be as violent and criminal as they were back in the day. In my opinion they are even more dangerous now, because young people are not fighting anymore. They are going straight to shooting. Some guys still join for protection, but it's more for popularity than anything. For example, back in 2004, rapper Lil Wayne added being a blood to his repertoire. Since he was so popular, everybody wanted to be a blood as well. Now, while he was a Blood commercially and it boosted sales because actual Blood gang members endorsed him, he had the resources to stay safe . It was just part of his image to add "gang member" along with having a being shot, being a gangster, and being a rapper. While gang culture is less intense these days, you still have to remember that joining a gang has real-life consequences. This is true even if you do it just to be cool. You are still at risk for retaliation because of association. Rival gangs don't care whether you actually did anything or not. They aren't going to give you a free pass. It doesn't matter if you change your life as an adult, those people that you were at war with might still be deep into that lifestyle. So you still have to watch your back. It's better to steer clear of gangs and their activities because if you join it will follow you for the rest of your life.

Sadly, gang culture is reinforced in the school system. If you're one of the smart guys, and I know you are, you go to school to get an education. At the same time, you know of a lot of kids who go to school to wreak havoc on rival gang members and bully other students not involved. So, while you're trying to get an education, you can't because the same pressures that apply out of school now apply in school. Questions will be asked even if you are not affiliated. Whatever neighborhood you live in, they might associate with the gang in that area. You sometimes don't have a choice. You could be wondering if you are going to end up in a fight after school because of gang affiliation or even just of assumed gang affiliation.

Although gangs are very prevalent in African American culture, there are ways to stay safe. The first and most important step is to become aware gang members, and their activities. If you can avoid these things, you are less likely to be approached by a gang or be a victim of a gang attack. Do not wear any kind of rag or colors associated with certain gangs. Do your research on gangs in your area to make sure you know where they are located and where they hang out. If you are ever approached, harmed, or threatened by a gang, tell law enforcement right away. It is not a sign of weakness to go to the police. You are just trying to keep yourself safe. Too many times, following the rules of the streets and "not snitching" is why criminals are still on the street hurting people. There is no doubt that some people are afraid to report gang activity for fear of retaliation. But in most cases, you can ask to remain anonymous. Most of the time nobody cares about wrongdoing until it affects them directly. Don't wait for that time. Be brave and change the narrative.

Education

"If you think education is expensive,
try ignorance."

— Andy McIntyre

I am a huge advocate of education. I think it is possibly the best way to spiral your way out of the poverty web. Education is proven to be the main way people can increase their lifetime earning potential and their socioeconomic status in life. As simple and as applicable as this may be, it's not easy for some to do, especially when you have so many things to worry about on top of getting an education. But if you are able to follow through, you have a chance on bettering your life.

Unfortunately, issues at home have a way of easing themselves into your daily life at school. There may be days when you might be thinking about what you are going to eat when you get home from school, or if there's even anything to eat at home. While you are at school, you know you don't have anything clean to wear tomorrow, so you plan to skip school. All of this is in your mind every day while being told you need to focus on school and get an education. With these kinds of challenges on your mind, it's not that easy to just go to school and focus on your studies.

The school system doesn't always do what it should to support your education. In many disadvantaged communities, the books and curriculum are not up to grade level at inner city schools as compared to suburban school. I experienced this firsthand when I went to inner city schools. We did a lot of work out of thin workbooks that were not challenging at all. When I changed to a school in the suburbs in sixth grade, we had thick comprehensive books for every subject. This is how I came to understand the resources in socio-economically challenged area schools are subpar compared to school districts in more affluent areas. When I began attending school in the suburbs as part of the VICC program, it was overwhelming. I remember thinking, "I don't understand this stuff." Interestingly, all my peers were working just fine. I decided to not raise my hand, because I didn't want other people to think I was different. The truth is, I hadn't been introduced to work that was actually at my true grade level until then. I had not been challenged this way before. The work was intense, and we had homework. I had never had homework before.

There were students who knew so much more than I did and I wanted to keep up with them, so I knew I had to get myself ready to learn so I wouldn't be even more behind. All of this taught me that you have to work hard if you want to succeed. I learned that if I didn't get it for myself, no one would be there to hold my hand and help me. At the same time, it felt so good being challenged to learn things quickly. I remember finally starting to understand the work and how excited I was. It made me feel like these people around me were not smarter or better than me, they just had a head start. I vowed to catch up and stay up. I brought everything I learned back to my community and started to devise my plan for success.

Getting an education is best way to get yourself out of poverty long term. Find a teacher, administrator, or mentor in the school. Tell them your plans to succeed, and ask if they can assist you. Tell them what worries you have. Ask what they can do to help. Adults want to see students do well. If you have the will to succeed, regardless of your circumstances, it is possible. You have to stay focused on your goals and try your best to avoid distractions and negativity.

Foods You Consume

Something that you might not put too much thought into is the food you consume. Having an education highlights how important eating healthy is in the grand scheme of learning and bettering yourself. I didn't pay much attention to what I was putting in my body until I got to college. People were watching their weight, counting calories and carbs, and eating vegetables willingly. They lectured me about how a healthy diet decreased your chances of getting certain diseases and how it was good for your overall health. Ideally, your parents would transfer this knowledge to you, but that isn't always the case if they aren't informed. For people living in poverty, high-quality, healthy food can be scarce. Also, healthier food is oftentimes more expensive than junk food. Chances are, though, if you are living in poverty, you are eating to survive, not to be healthy.

When money is available to buy food, usually an abundance of snacks are purchased, including chips, sodas, and snack cakes which are all poor in nutriational value. I will be the first to admit that these foods taste good and are packed with carbohydrates, so you fill full after eating them. Who doesn't want to fill full? Your meals may also resemble low-cost frozen pizzas, ramen noodles, and various quick and easy micro-wavable meals. Before being introduced to a healthier lifestyle while in college, these are the types of foods I was used to eating. Interestingly, these are also the foods that lead to high blood pressure, high cho-lesterol, and heart disease; diseases that kill so many living in poverty. But, while in college, I learned about nutrition and started eating balanced meals and working out. I then began to track my calorie intake, watch my weight, and make sure I consumed more fruits and vegetables.

When you eat, you want to feel good, so you usually make poor choices for meals. Eating healthy doesn't benefit you, because you just want something that fills your stomach now. Pizza taste better and leaves you more satisfied than salad so naturally who wouldn't choose that. The future is later, so you will deal with it then. Well, how many people in your community do you know have had any of the health conditions mentioned? Good health starts with what you decide to put in your body. You have to implement changes now while you're young so you won't regret it later. You don't take into account that bad dietary choices will catch up with you over time. So just take a look what you consume and figure out if there are healthier options. These high calorie, fat, sugar, and sodium packed items aren't entirely bought by choice either; they are the most accessible, because you are living in a food desert.

Food desert is defined as "an urban area in which it is difficult to buy affordable or good quality fresh foods." I used to wonder why people of other races would jog and eat healthy. I would say to myself, "They must not like the taste of good food." In reality, the food I thought was good was actually bad for me. But it was cheap, accessible, and tasted great to me. If my parents are eating it, why can't I eat it? It's hard to see something wrong with something everybody is doing around you. So, don't feel bad if this sounds like you.

With that being said, I'm going to share some information with you about eating right. A healthier diet leads to weight loss, better mood, reduced risk of cancer, stroke prevention, and better heart health. Limiting your meat consumption and eating plenty of fruits and vegetables can lead to longer life expectancy. Not only is it good for your body, but it's also good for your mental well-being. You maintain a certain sense of pride and esteem when you are filtering what you put into your body. Things you can do to ensure better health is monitor your daily salt, sugar, and fat intake. Too much salt can lead to hypertension, high blood pressure, and even stroke. Too much sugar can lead to obesity and diabetes. Too much fat can lead to increased cholesterol levels, obesity, heart disease, certain cancers, and diabetes. Often times, the foods we love so much contain a mixture of all three of these things. You don't have to completely stop eating high salt, fat, and sugary foods, but you should only consume them in moderation. These health tips are not something to consider just when you're older. A buildup of unhealthy choices leads to complications later. Control it while you are young so that you will have a head start on good health.

Mentality

The basic human needs, as stated by Maslow, are physiological, safety, love, esteem, and self-actualization. Physiological and safety needs are among the most important because they heavily influence the last three. The first order of needs to be met are the physiological ones. This includes air, water, food, shelter, sleep, clothing, and reproduction. The important ones to pay attention to are water, food, and shelter. If you have not satisfied or don't have your basic physiological needs met, it's impossible to move on to the next category. You are still fighting a battle to have stable food and shelter. If someone is extremely hungry, it is hard for them to focus on anything other than their next meal.

There have been times in my life when we didn't have a lot of food, so I enjoyed going to school for breakfast and lunch. I remember thinking about what we would have for dinner later that night all through the school day. If there even was going to be dinner. It bombarded all of my thoughts, and I couldn't pay attention. Whatever the teacher was talking about did not matter, because she wasn't feeding me. She is not real to me. She's just a lady at the school who's always trying to tell me what to do. In reality, this is a teacher who is trying to help me learn things so I would have a chance to be successful in the future. But with a hungry stomach, my only care was about the present and the future as it related to food, my immediate physiological need. So, if your basic needs aren't met, you are not going to be engaged in school. So Being in your same shoes really not paying attention to my teachers because I had so much going on is understandable. Even now while working in the schools I am aware of students unmotivated to learn, but I strive to teach you balance. What is happening now in your life doesn't have to be forever. Let's address your issues and communicate what will help you to focus.

The next category of needs is safety. This includes personal security, employment, resources, and health. Your mother might be employed, but because of a lack of education and skills, she may earn very low wages and the family may not have health insurance. This need not being met puts even more stress on her, which will ultimately affects you and the rest of your family. If you see that your parents are struggling and can barely help themselves, you may adopt the mindset to fend for yourself. With scarce resources available, you may be forced to venture on your own to find things such as food and shelter. You might have the right mind or intentions to go and work for what you want. But what if that job takes too long to call back? What if you are hungry right now, but have no money to feed yourself? In the absence of a vital resources, stable housing, and a safe neighborhood, things can quickly fall apart.

Being rich is a reality. Being middle class is a reality. Being poor is an unfortunate reality. The mindset in each class is drastically different, though. A rich person doesn't have to wonder where they are staying, because their house, car, and all bills are paid in totality. They might have a personal chef cook for them every night, a refrigerator full of food, or money to go out to eat every night. There are no worries. A middle-class family may have a note on a house and car, but income is enough to take care of this. They may even have a savings account to pay for unexpected expenses. The poor family, however, does not enough money to buy or finance a car. If they can afford one, it will be a late model, which is bound to have complications soon. There is no savings account available to take care of breakdowns. Not having backup means these situations cause more stress, anger, and anxiety. These are the stressors that parents have to deal with. And often, you the child, may feel pressured to help out.

As a young man, you may be willing to go and work for what you want, but sometimes the job takes too long to call back. When everything seems to keep failing and you are tired of trying and being disappointed, you begin to take on a survival mode mentality. This means you are just trying to get through the day and have no long-term plan. You don't care about morality, because you don't live by many. The world has been so savage to you why not carry the same attitude? You only focus on the need to survive and by any means necessary. Not until you are out of survival mode does the healthy ability to make decisions return. Then, you're able to start thinking about right and wrong. Out of desperation, you might make the mistake of stealing or robbing someone. Your mind might convince you that there is no other way of getting what you need. If the only way you have seen people obtain material desires or personal success is through selling drugs, robbing, and stealing, you might think these are the only options you have to fall back on. None of these things are acceptable means of getting what you want though. The problem is if no one knows what you are going through, how can they help? Too many times I was too afraid or embarrassed to ask for help when I needed it. I want you to think before you make a bad decision out of desperation. You can't let being in an inconvenient situation put you in an even worse situation by acting out irrationally.

So, what do you do to change your mentality? Well, first of all, you consider all the negatives that are going on in your life. Then, you devise a plan.

When I was growing up, we had to find out where food pantries were by looking at the news, reading newspapers or by word of mouth. These days, any-one can find out about places to get food by going online. There are charities on social media displaying their food pantries and giveaways. There are good Samaritans, also, who randomly post that they are serving free lunch and dinner to those in need out of the kindness of their heart. You have resources readily available and more easily accessible than ever. Schools provide food bags to children who may be in need of them. Your school social worker or principal should be able to provide you with resources, as well. Never compromise your freedom by making bad choices to obtain things you need, like food.

As a child or teenager, you can't control where you live. That is usually determined by your family's income and qualifications. If your family is only able to live in poverty-stricken areas, you have to accept that and begin your process toward improvement. What you have to do is not become susceptible to things you see and hear. Everybody is aware that their situation isn't the best; that's why they are living there. You may witness a lot of negativity around you. Do not let that become you. Your goal is to stay away from negative people and not get caught in unnecessary drama. Keep busy inside the house and stay with your family. I stress this, because if you befriend certain negative people, you may regret it later on. The moment you all fall out, they still know a lot about you and can use that to threaten or manipulate you. It's okay to speak and be cordial, but do not try to get involved. Find friends who have the same ambitions as you do, and cling on to each other.

Chapter 2 ‖ Ok, What About the Police?

As a teenager growing up in St. Louis City, I would walk around the neighborhood with friends. Every time we saw the police, we were nervous. We knew they would try to stop and harass us for no reason. They would ask us what we were doing, where we were going, and if we had drugs on us. We were literally just boys walking, talking, and having a good time. We did nothing to warrant their attention, yet they bothered us because they could.

"I don't like the police"

This is the way that young black men feel but also how a lot of black people feel, in general. And I get it. With so many examples of how police have wrongly assaulted, shot, or killed black people, even when they are compliant, the mistreatment of black people by police is obvious to almost everyone, except the police. It is sickening, shameful, and unjust. How could one ever be expected to trust someone who doesn't have their best interests in mind, especially when skin color is the main motivating factor? How can you trust or believe someone can help you when they are judging you before they even get to know you? There have been so many incidents of black people calling the police to report a crime or for help in settling a disagreement, only to get harassed by them. When calling law enforcement also means you could be putting yourself in danger, it feels like a lose-lose situation. There is no hiding the fact that there is a tremulous relationship problem between blacks and law enforcement, especially in the urban areas.

You may feel helpless, as if no matter what you say or do, the police are going to do what they want to anyway. The sheer reality of living in a low-income neighborhood might be cause police officers to assume you are a criminal, even though you are not a bad person. Sadly, the bad behaviors of a few in a group dictate how the whole group is perceived. It is not the right mentality to have, but unfortunately, it happens.

The people who are supposed to protect and serve us are the ones we need protection from. Although I can't say all police are like this, the ones who are, end up giving those good officers a bad reputation.

> *"There are, fundamentally, two ways*
> *you can experience the police in*
> *America: as the people you call when*
> *there's a problem, the nice man in*
> *uniform who pats a toddler on his head*
> *and has an easy smile for the old lady*
> *as she buys her coffee. For others, the*
> *police are the people who are called on*

them. They are the ominous knock on the door, the sudden flashlight in the face, the barked orders.

Depending on who you are, the sight of an officer can produce either a warm sense of safety and contentment or a plummeting feeling of terror."

— Chris L. Hayes, A Colony in a Nation

How the police think

The media is a very important contributor to how the world shapes its views of black people. It is further enforced and influenced by videos of interactions on the internet and social media. More often than not, black people are portrayed as violent, aggressive, un-educated, and non-law abiding. If you didn't grow up around the people you are policing, it's impossible to know what they really are like. *Some police rely mostly on what they hear and see before even trying to establish a relationship with the community they are policing.* That's where the big disconnect is. Not all officers, but some, will assume you don't care about your life because you live in a poverty-stricken community. They think that if you did care, you wouldn't live there. They assume you don't value anything, that you want to be a criminal. The media says it, so it must be true. That is the conclusion they come to in their heads.

Police officers get away with killing black people all the time on television, so no one must care about them. This does not just apply to law enforcement. The way the media portrays young black men as erratic, misbehaved, and dangerous forms the opinions of the masses. So, you have to realize off the bat the odds are not in your favor when faced with a confrontation. You are black, so you are already assumed to be the aggressor in most cases.

Police officers put their lives on the line every day when they go to work. When put in hostile situations, combined with the perception that blacks are violent animals and don't care about their lives, some police feel no remorse about using deadly force. They may feel as if it's either kill or be killed. That mentality is not the problem, though, when faced with a hostile or deadly situation. The problem is when officers go into a situation ready to kill or use excessive force instead of de-escalation attempts, because of a bias they already have about a certain group of people.

How to survive

Being a young black male living in America means having a target on your back at all times. You will, no doubt, have to encounter good and bad police. You will also come into contact with police officers who try to take advantage of their authority. No matter which type of police officer you encounter, you need to be able to handle yourself accordingly. Police are trained to handle situations a certain way and according to protocol. Even though they are trained to behave and do things a certain way, it doesn't necessarily mean they will. This can be frustrating as a black man, because you are usually the one who they discriminate against and use ill will against.

A lot of times, black people will try to handle court on the streets, and that's the worst way to go about it. If you encounter an officer who is speaking to you in a rude and disrespectful way, or harassing you for no reason, and you know you haven't done anything wrong, just stay calm and comply with whatever he or she is asking. Watch your words, your body language, and your emotions. If you get hostile right back with them, because you know you are right, they now have a reason to further harass you. Just comply if you are pulled over and asked for your identification. Even if they insist on checking your vehicle, allow them to do it. You can report this later or get a lawyer to press charges on your behalf. But for now, just comply to avoid any other negative actions. As a man, it is hard to do what an officer or any other man tells you to do. But in the event of being stopped by the police, your compliance could be the difference between life or death…yours!

Keep your hands in plain sight so that the police can see your hands at all times. The importance of this was illustrated in the 2016 incident involving Philando Castile. After being pulled over for a traffic violation, Philando followed the officer's direction to retrieve his identification. He had told the officer he had a gun on him and that he had a license to carry.

The officer got on high alert after he was told that. But that was not because of the gun. It was because Philando was black and had a gun. The officer, assuming Philando to be dangerous, immediately became anxious. The officer told Philando to show him his license and registration. Upon reaching for said items in the glove compartment, Philando was shot numerous times. The officer mistakenly thought he was reaching for the gun, but he was retrieving the documents the officer had requested. The gun was actually in Philando's pocket. He was shot, despite the fact that he was doing the right thing. What chance will you have by not complying?

Incidents like this show that you have to be even more careful when put in situations with the police. If you are not clear on what an officer wants you to do, ask again to be clear. If an officer asks you to retrieve something, ask them how they want you to do it. Offer them the opportunity to check it themselves if you feel harm may come to you if you make any sudden moves. Do what you feel will result in the safest outcome for yourself. Do not run, even if you are afraid of the police. If you are running, they will assume you have something dangerous and are trying to hide it. Stay calm and remain in control. Is arguing your point right now worth being locked up, physically assaulted, or killed? These are the questions you have to ask yourself when you encounter these situations.

If you feel that your rights have been violated, you and your parents have the right to file a formal complaint with your local police jurisdiction. You want to be living to have a chance to argue your point in a courtroom. That's the responsible way to handle it. You can't argue with a police officer on the streets and expect to win. Don't let pride interfere with you making rational decisions to keep yourself safe.

Chapter 3 ‖ Social Media: A Two-Way Sword

Social media has become the most influential wave of the present day. We no longer look to traditional news channels to find out what's going on in sports, politics, and entertainment. We just slide over to our Twitter and Facebook pages to get the scoop. Whether we want to admit it or not, social media is where everyone gets most of their information about everything. Some say that if it isn't posted on social media, it didn't happen. That said, many of the behaviors we display, the things we buy, and the lifestyle we aspire to live are influenced by our favorite people on Instagram, Twitter, or Facebook. That includes the influence of athletes and rappers on the psyche of young black men. Rap culture is where the majority of people form opinions of how young black men are and behave. Rap and hip hop are the most popular genres of music in the world today. That means a huge population of people are listening to music and watching the artists. Oftentimes, rappers portray a gangster image to sell records. The more chains, rings, designer clothes and cars they exhibit, the more believable they are. What most young black men don't realize, however, is that perception is not reality.

Perception vs. Reality

A Wikipedia search for most rappers would reveal that many were former high school athletes, graduated high school, and/or attended college. A lot of rappers grew up in two-parent households and did not live a bad life at all. They were afforded the resources to fund a rap career. Rapper Blueface, for example, led his high school football team to a championship and went on to play in college. Yet, most fans know him for his gangster rap lyrics. He does not choose to rap about his real upbringing, because it's not conducive to his rap career. Violence and sex sells, so that's exactly what he raps about. In a 2019 article in Complex magazine, written by Fnr Tigg, Blueface says, "Invest in yaself. A chain is more than a chain, and this rap shyt, it's all about da image. It's not about how good you rap or how good you freestyle. It's 2020; it's a popularity contest. You get paid based off how cool you look an' how much you appeal to your fan base. It's a new rapper every 5 min; you gotta stick if you want longevity in this shyt. Do you think people notice if you don't have a chain?"

He is explaining that rap is all about looking cool to be popular. So many young men take these rappers' lives to be real and desire to emulate them. While these rappers are paid and able to portray an image, you face real-life consequences of prison or death trying to be like them. Don't risk your life or freedom trying to be like your favorite rapper. Rapping is entertainment. These are people that are making a very comfortable living off your money. Instead, get an education. It's fine if you want to be a rapper, too, but understand that emulating the lifestyle they portray on television will not get you there. If they really did all these crimes they talk about, shouldn't the police be knocking at their door right now? Also, why would you tell on yourself to the world? It's evident that it's just storytelling to a nice beat. Enjoy it as just that.

Social media is the best invention ever

One positive thing social media has done is provided new ways for not only young black men but everyone to make money legally. I am very excited about that. Rapping is one of those ways. Now, more than ever, it is easier and cheaper to make a beat, produce a song, and shoot a video. You can self-promote your music on all social media sites for free. All you have to do is be a little creative and get friends to like and share your content. Then, you're well on your way! You don't have to wait until you're 15 or 16 to get a job anymore.

There are so many lucrative ways to make money at any age. And that doesn't just apply to rap. You can make videos on YouTube, start a blog, run a podcast, or start a small business out of your house. There is an 8-year-old YouTube star named Ryan Kaji. He started a channel in 2015 making five-minute toy unboxing videos. His page eventually grew in views and subscribers. He earned around

$22 million in 2019. Even as an athlete, you don't have to wait to hopefully be seen to be recruited. You can now make highlight tapes of your best plays and send them to colleges. Self-marketing is the new wave, and the possibilities are endless. If you find something you really like to do, you can make it profitable. There are so many ways to use social media to promote yourself to gain fame and fortune, without solely depending on the usual rapper or ball player way out. Social media exposes you to a new world. Technology is your best friend. Well, that is, until it isn't.

I hate social media

Every adult has been young before. And every adult has made some terrible decisions. The thing is, when your parents and other adults made mistakes, it was between the people that were involved to rectify and fix it. These days, when people have problems, they use an outlet such as social media to rant about it. Sometimes, young people make status updates about a particular person and say some not-so-nice things. When you do that, you are drawing everyone that follows you into your problems. When this happens, you blow it out of proportion and make a bigger feud than necessary. You could have addressed the person face to face. This isn't even the biggest problem, though.

Once you publish something on the internet, it belongs to the internet forever. People can pull your tweet, Instagram, or Facebook post up years from now. What if somebody takes a picture of your Facebook status to send to someone? What if an employer wants to know more about you before they hire you, and they find your status about wanting to fight someone? What if you post that you don't like a certain group of people and they find that tweet? It's not going to look good on you. Even if you were young, uneducated, and foolish back then, your status is still there. You are going to have to explain your behavior to an employer. It seems like every week a new celebrity's racist, hateful, homophobic, or insensitive tweets arise out of nowhere. Comedian, Kevin hart, was supposed to host the 2019 Oscars ceremony before near-decade-old homophobic tweets of his emerged. He was forced to give an explanation for these tweets. It's true that the tweets were ten years old. He may not even feel the same way now, but people wanted him to apologize for them. The same thing applies to pictures and videos. Make sure you aren't posting offensive, violent, derogatory, or sexually explicit images and videos of yourself or anyone else. Be careful about what you post on the internet. It will follow you.

Chapter 4 ‖ Education

Now, I'm going to tell you something that a lot of people probably wouldn't agree with. I do not believe going to college is as necessary as it used to be in order for you to be successful. Look at the surge in entrepreneurship in the economy. To be an entrepreneur means to organize and operate your own business. Looking back, I wish I had more information about going to college, such as cost, degree programs, and job outlook. Many jobs that used to require a degree only require a high school education or some college credits now. But I went to college. I did want to be better educated, but I went mostly because I was told it would increase my earning potential.

Look around you right now. Young people are making money and becoming well off or getting rich before they even reach high school. You could very well be so innovative you start your own business and succeed without ever needing to go to school. Of course, this route won't be easy or profitable for everyone. Just know the option is there. Now, more than ever, knowledge and information is at your fingertips. You can look on YouTube to learn how to do practically anything. You can find the answer to any question you want by typing it into a Google search. The days of having to read big books as the only source for information are gone. Technology has enabled new, faster, and more creative ways to make money. If you find something that people want, and can provide it faster, with better quality, and for cheaper, you are well on your way!

The basics: Graduating high school

If you have had a difficult and not-so-pleasant upbringing, school might be the last thing on your mind. But getting an education is the most important thing you can do. By education, I mean you don't necessarily have to go to college. Sadly, though, a lot of young people aren't even graduating from high school or middle school. No matter how street smart you think you are, that is not a skill that's going to transfer over to the real world. Who is going to hire someone who can't fill out an application because of their inability to read? What if you are required to work the register but don't know how to count money correctly? If you are not happy with the way you are living now and want it to change, obtaining at minimum a high school diploma is the best route. Chances are, if you haven't completed high school, you won't be able to apply for most entry level positions anywhere. Don't limit your possibilities from the gate. In high school you get a chance to think about what you really want to do with your life. If you are not sure you have plenty of educators to assist you. Even if you don't want to pursue a college degree after high school, use it to hone skills you will need for the path you chose to take.

The college experience

Nothing quite changed my life as much as my first year of college. I was so excited, but scared at the same time. I had to learn how to get to all these classes by myself, and I needed help. Everybody was walking fast, like they were in a rush. I felt helpless and out of place, and I just wanted to go home. It seemed like everybody knew what they were doing, and I, being the inner-city kid, was out of place. Even the other black colleagues at school knew where to go and what to do.

As I began to meet people, I started to realize that a huge majority of my black colleagues had not grown up in the same socioeconomically disadvantaged areas as I had. They were raised in the suburbs. Prior to that experience, I never knew black people could have money and live in affluent areas. I was completely thrown off when I saw white and black people talking and getting along. In my neighborhood, white people would walk away from groups of blacks, in fear they would get robbed or assaulted. I learned to accept a world I wasn't used to, and it made me mad. I was mad because, growing up in my neighborhood, I wasn't exposed to anything else. That environment kept me trapped in a certain mindset. I had been living and thinking all wrong. Thankfully, in college, I ended up having friends of all races that I could trust and count on. They taught me things about life I never knew. I never cared about my health or physical fitness, but in college it was everyone's top focus after academics. I was informed on how eating healthy can increase your lifespan while improving your sense of self. Being health conscious has so many benefits. It didn't take long before I was hooked. Till this day, I stress that working out increases your self-esteem and helps you relieve stress.

These new friends showed me that if you work hard, you can get a lot more out of life. I was exposed to intelligent, progressive, and ambitious people I would have never met had I not gone to college. As of right now, I have friends who are millionaires, doctors, lawyers, popular influencers with over a million followers, and co-hosts on Yahoo Sports whose personal phone numbers I can call right now. Oh, and would you believe all these people are black? This shows you that getting an education is important, but also the connections you build through the process are priceless.

I just explained why college was so influential for me, and it can be for you, as well. My main reason for going was because when I was growing up, I was taught that if you want to better your life, you should go to college, get a degree, and find a job. When you find that job, you need to work 30-plus years until you retire. That sounded great back then. But in 2020, jobs are hard to come by, and degrees don't produce the salaries they used to. Making $30,000 a year for a single person was considered doing well 20 years ago. Now, that's just enough to get by. The price of everything has risen since then, including food, housing, and college expenses.

Some would say that going to college is a waste of time, because what you earn will not be enough to compensate for the student loans you took out. People are having to work two and three jobs to get by now. It's hard. But while you're young, you need to be able to internalize this valuable information given to you by adults looking out for you. I didn't have anyone to tell me this information, and the people who did had very little education about the specifics. If you are able to go to college, pick a specialized occupation that can sustain loan repayments, such as a doctor, lawyer, engineer, or software developer. This is not to say you can't go to school for anything else. In fact, you should only go to school for whatever major interests you. But the major you want to pursue might not have a high-paying salary. It is important, though, if you want to make a certain amount of money, you research career paths that provide that desired salary. Another important thing you should research is what school you will attend, because most offer the same degree program, but at different tuition prices. A private college may cost $30,000 a year to attend; whereas you could attend a state school and pay half that a year for the same degree. You have to make important decisions when it comes to your education. This is information that a guidance counselor in school might give you.

Chapter 5 ‖ Church

Christianity holds a historical and definite influence in the African American community. Many find comfort in the biblical messages that promote and evoke feelings of spirituality, repentance, and deliverance. From a historical standpoint, religion helped strengthen blacks and establish cohesiveness during the Civil Rights Movement. Things were difficult for black people during those times. Having church, singing hymns, and praising God seemed to put people at ease. With no other outlet to voice frustrations safely, church provided a community of individuals, all facing the same struggles, a place to confide in and comfort one another. It was a uniting force that helped our people overcome so many obstacles.

Growing up, I saw a lot of churches in my neighborhood. I didn't understand who had the money to fund all these churches to be built and how they were sustained. From my experience, the majority of the people attending the church were poor, distressed, and needing of assistance. I remember saying to myself, "For all the bad things going on, you would think all these churches would make the area better." Well, at least that's what I hoped for. The thing is, growing up, I attended church regularly and accepted the beliefs and principles they taught me. I saw people who frequented church regularly, who were at their wits end with troubles in life, but kept coming just looking for some sign of hope. People filling the pews that had been through so much that they couldn't take it anymore. Their last resort was church. It was like after service they were reset. They could go back out and deal with the cold and harsh world. I saw the pastor anoint their heads, and they were filled with the Holy Ghost. Church was a place of worship, to get together, talk about the hard times, and share how God got them through. No matter what the discussion was, the last words leaving the conversation would be, "God is good, have faith, and your blessing is coming." It was so rehearsed, I don't even know if some people believed it or whether they were just used to saying it out of common courtesy or habit.

I noticed something while they were talking. It was the uncanny way they would refer to God about even the simplest occurrence. For example, every time somebody said something good happened to them, the response was, "Thank God" or "The Lord did it." Somebody would say, "I found a dollar on the floor" or, "Whoops, I almost fell out the car, but the Lord caught me." I could tell the older people who were saying this didn't really believe God did it. They were just so used to hearing it and saying it that it had become routine. I don't believe everything that happens big or small was because of God.

People were so dependent on God doing things for them that they failed to rely on themselves to do something. Consider this example. Did you get the job because you presented yourself well, met all the qualifications, and did an excellent job answering the questions? Or did none of that matter and God made it happen? I saw the flaw in logic in the church as a young man coming up. I saw that a lot of people there just wanted to believe, and some needed a reason to explain the life of despair they are living in. A lot of pastors would preach that things would get better. Just hope. Just pray. Just stay strong. I believe you should do all those things, as well, but what about some practical knowledge to help their situation? If he or she encouraged struggling church members to go back to school to further their education, apply at higher-paying jobs, or offer assistance to help manage money, then that would be more effective than saying stay hopeful.

Church as crutch

"For as the body without the spirit is dead, so faith without works is dead also."

— James 2:26

This scripture says to me that you can have all the faith you want, but if you don't put in the work, nothing is going to come of it. This is the problem in the church that hurts the people. Too much ranting about faith and not enough doing on the behalf of the people. That's not the members' fault though. After all, they are just following their leader. What should be taught in the church are actual applications that could improve one's status, but these things were never talked about. I felt like the congregation of people wanted fast answers and they remedied that by saying, "Just pray, Things will get better." But there were no instructions or guidance on how to make things better.

Church, no doubt, gave people a reason to stay hopeful. But it failed to prepare people to be better. For this reason, I believe young people don't feel the need to go to church. It does not fulfill a purpose. I also noticed people would be in church, but then would leave for a couple months to sin. Then, when they would come back, they were praised for beating the devil. This behavior would happen repeatedly. It became a joke to me at one point in time. I'm not saying every church experience is like this, but the purpose it once served for the good has been severely altered these days. It was evident to me that church was a place people could come for hope, repentance, and forgiveness. But that is now being taken for granted because people want to be holy for a couple months, leave to have fun, and then come back to repent. That's' how I view church these days.

I've always said religion is functional. Its purpose is to halt you from doing bad things in exchange for earning a ticket to heaven. If not for religion in underprivileged communities, more robberies, killings, and crimes would occur. People would lose hope and feel no one cares about them. In this instance church or religion serves its purpose. Religion tries to instill good morals in you to keep you away from what you really want to do when placed in a bad situation, which is engaging in illegal activities to fulfill your needs.

A challenge to outdated principles

The old-school church values of the past were starting to be questioned by my generation. What the church stood for was losing its power. There were too many rules, and I needed answers. Did everything in the Bible really happen or is it just a bunch of fables meant to teach a lesson? If I don't pay tithes will I not be allowed in heaven? Why is everybody in the church poor but people who don't even attend church aren't? Make this make sense. It's almost as if the churches in the black community were saying that you have to struggle in this life to earn your way into heaven. Well, is it ok to not struggle and make it to heaven too? If you were doing well you were looked at as not being humble and also expected to contribute more to the church. All these unwritten rules and expectations. These are all the questions I had growing up in the church, but I just decided to keep observing.

Fast forward to present day; this is why the church isn't as effective as it used to be to change young black men. As a young man, I refused to believe without trying to apply some knowledge to what I was hearing and seeing. I was one of the few who said, "I am not about to follow along just because that's what you're supposed to do." If it doesn't make sense, it doesn't make sense. I had questions and needed to find out things for myself. I guess you can say I was rebellious, but I was one of the first in my generation to challenge these principles I had grown to know. I was considered odd and defiant.

Today's young people will challenge everything and demand answers. If you can't find it or make sense, they move on. They won't tolerate, racism, discrimination, inequality, unequal pay, bullying, or disrespect. They have a voice these days and will use it. The old institution of church and religion encourages followers to be quiet, vigilant, obedient, love thy neighbors, and pray to solve issues. This is another reason why the church has lost its influence on young people. The old-school values don't align with the times we are living in. Just as people want new, young leadership in political parties to bring new ideas, the church needs the same type of restructuring.

Meanwhile, some wealthier people do not attend church. They may not even believe in God. This is what made me come to the conclusion that religion they teach in the church is there to help poor people feel better, because their situations are unfortunate. When you don't need anyone for anything, it can be hard to see why you would worship someone. If wealthy people have money and don't attend church, but poor people do go to church faithfully and don't have money, something is not adding up. That's a simplistic way to put it but if you already have things, you don't necessarily have to pray and hope to get things. I questioned what the rich are doing that's so different from what the poor do. I realized that the old institutions and beliefs about church, and the purpose it's supposed to serve, are what keep people stagnant. They aren't preaching growth; they are preaching hope. You can hope all you want for a better job, but you won't get one unless you go find it. People in church need to be taught valuable life skills, given resources, and the importance of education stressed to them.

While I may have conflicting opinions about religion and its practices compared to others, I do think attending church has its benefits. As a young man growing up in church, I learned how to remember and recite long speeches. I learned that it was morally right to do the right thing, to not sin, and to help others in need. We were one of the families in need, and the church helped us. When things got hard, I wanted to feel safe. Church did that for me. The preacher, the missionaries, and the mothers would always call me smart and say I was going to be somebody important. It was a confidence booster and honestly stuck with me my whole life. Because of that, I encourage you to attend church. There are some good men in there who can teach how you how to walk, talk, and carry yourself as a young man. Attend church and take what you need from it. You won't find everything you need in church, but you will learn some valuable information regarding integrity, honesty, and being a good person.

Chapter 6 ‖ Five Life Tips to Follow as a Man

As a black man growing up, I was constantly reminded of the uphill struggle I was facing. It was all a result of my race. I knew that my poor socioeconomic status growing up would shape my outlook on life. I also knew I had to do something about it by gaining an education and not falling victim to the chaos I was surrounded by. I knew the decisions I made, whether positive or negative, would affect me the rest of my life. I saw that my circumstances could make me bitter and hopeless, but I fought against it.

Some people want you to be down and stay down. You don't have to. I encourage you to find that special someone; a person to latch onto for guidance. Never be afraid to ask for help. That's the first step to moving out of your comfort zone. Someone saw something special in me and decided to help me. Do not place all blame on society. Instead, let it be the reason you are willing to obtain more. Conquer all and tell your story. Reach out to another brother and show them what they are capable of.

Finances and spending

One thing I have noticed is how many members of our community misuse their funds. When people receive their check, they will buy things they want instead of taking care of what they need. Their needs include paying rent, utilities, and other bills. Bills should be taken care of first. People feel they have worked hard the whole week, so they deserve to splurge on themselves. The problem is, splurging on yourself will bring temporary happiness but will leave you in debt and cause you to be stressed. The following week, bills are due that you could have paid, but you bought things you wanted with the money. That's the problem. People living in poverty are constantly putting themselves in a bind by making poor financial decisions.

This is a problem that the black community faces. It is not just black males. It's perfectly fine to want to look good, dress well, smell good, and drive a nice car. But, if these expenses are putting you behind in paying bills, or you can't afford it, then what's the point? Are you going to have a $500 outfit on while you are picking up furniture outside the house you got evicted from? Financial literacy is something that black men aren't taught growing up, because money is scarce. So, when we get money, we are excited and want to spend it.

There are ways to make your money work for you through saving, investing, stocks and bonds, and eliminating debt. Having money in your savings account stacked up for hard times feels way better than spending it on unnecessary items. Having some savings also gives you peace of mind. Try to ensure you are allocating your funds to the best of your ability. When you receive money—maybe a paycheck, income tax refund, or endowment—make it your duty to pay your bills first. If you have money left over, put it in a savings account. In this tough economy, no job is guaranteed. Therefore, if something happens with your employment, or if an emergency arises, you are prepared.

Appearance

You're not supposed to judge a book by its cover. But, if we're being honest, you have to make some assumptions about people you encounter. In the case of a black male, there are stereotypes that are assumed to be true by people because of the way you present yourself. Here are a few simple suggestions that will come in handy in presenting yourself more professionally and respectfully.

You should strive to wear clothes that fit your body. Fitted clothing looks better than baggy clothes, and compliment your physique. It is very necessary to wear a belt with your pants to avoid having to keep pulling your pants up. Make sure you own dress clothes to be prepared for formal events, such as weddings, banquets, church, and interviews. A clean shave can go a long way with making you appear well kept. If you are dressed nicely, having a good smelling cologne enhances your image even more. Lastly, women respect a well-dressed, well-kept man. You exude confidence and class. People compliment you and take you more seriously when you are well put together.

Doctor

When black men go to the doctor, it's usually because the symptoms of whatever illness they have been dealing with have become overbearingly painful and they can't take it anymore. Sadly, this is the reason why black men have one of the shortest life spans compared to men of other races. We simply don't go to the doctor early enough to catch signs of completely preventable conditions. In our culture, if something hurts, we are more likely told to "tough it out" or to go to sleep and see if it gets better. Some men are afraid to go to the doctor because they feel they will be diagnosed with something, so they would rather not go. Regardless of the reasons, you need to go annually to get yourself checked out. A lot of the time, you may be fine. But, you don't want to find out that if you would have seen the doctor sooner, you could have prevented a chronic illness.

Relationships with women

It's a "badge of recognition" to a lot of immature and simple-minded men that more women you get with the more of a man you are. This could not be further from the truth. You define a man by his character, principles, and morals. Sleeping with a bunch of women just in-creases your chances of getting a woman pregnant and /or contracting a sexually transmitted disease (STD). Women are to be adored, admired, and respected. They are not to be treated however you feel and then on to the next. Ask yourself would you like it if your sister, mother, or female family member was treated as such? Just something to remember and think about.

Father your children

I feel like this is a given, but judging by all the single black mothers out there, it isn't. If you have a baby, you need to man-up and take responsibility for the life you helped bring in this world. You might not have been prepared, but neither was the mother, in most cases. You need to get prepared. So many young men enter the system at a young age, because they don't have male guidance at home. When I say enter the system I mean committing crimes and being entered into the juvenile court system. Once you start that you get used to being locked up and are already being molded into the culture of corrections. A lot of young men don't know how they should look, act, or behave. They end up looking for guidance elsewhere, and that's usually in people who are less than admirable. You may not have had your father in your life. So, think about how that made you feel. Do you want your child to feel the same way about you as you felt about your absent father? Break the cycle. Be the father to your family.

Company you keep

I have given you many tools to aid you in navigating life's obstacles and to be successful. None of that matters if you choose to hang around people who lack the same ambition as you. I love the saying by Confucius, "If you are the smartest person in the room, you're in the wrong room." This is basically saying that if you want to keep growing and prospering, you have to surround yourself with like-minded people. Understand that when you are bettering yourself, some people are not going to be on board with that. Some people will praise you for it, while others will think that you believe you're better than they are. Don't be afraid to leave the ones behind who have negative things to say about your vision and moves.

Chapter 7 ‖ Tips for Educators and Parents

Preparing at risk children to be functional members of society requires adults to teach discipline, structure, and then education. Adults should strive to address behaviors and come to a solution to manage young people more effectively. In turn, the fewer behaviors young people display, the more concentrated and attentive they will be, and the more one-on-one time will be available to work with them. When young people feel their needs are being addressed, or at least talked about, they are more open and trusting and willing to listen to what adults have to say. You have to build rapport with children, just like you have to with adults, for them to trust and open up to you. This is when you emphasize how obtaining an education will assist them in bettering themselves and their families in the future

Especially when I'm talking to young black boys, I make sure to teach discipline and structure first. With the state of young black men in America and the senseless killings by the police, as well as black on black crime, emphasizing they practice restraint in being verbally and physically aggressive is key. What importance is getting an education if they aren't alive to use it? You can teach these young men how to read, write, and do math, but as soon as they get into a confrontation with a police officer or another peer in the neighborhood, their life could be over right then and there. Learning math, science, and social studies did not prepare them to effectively handle themselves when approached by the police. While education is extremely important, societal hurdles they are dealing with have to be addressed, for their safety and also to gain trust. After rapport is built with student chances are they are more willing to listen.

Structure is needed to raise young black men effectively and that's what a father being present in the home provides. While working at juveniles and group homes for boys, I found out that these guys appreciated having expectations and rules to follow. I've come to recognize that this system works to deter young men from making bad decisions. Not only that, they appreciated it and felt they had "purpose" and really took their jobs to heart. It's only when they had free time to meddle around that fights, arguments, and chaos ensue. When there are no consequences for their actions and they get rewarded for doing the bare minimum, they feel they can get away with anything and have low expectations for themselves. Then, they go out in the world thinking they can do and say whatever they want to anybody, and hit a brick wall. Unfortunately, that wall may be death or jail. That's why it is important to find a mentor or positive male role model to teach your students, sons, nephews, or young men in your life how to conduct themselves. Learning to exercise discipline and getting an education are equally important in ensuring the safety of these young men. What you learn in school will assist you in obtaining a more comfortable life. How you carry yourself will keep you safe and out of harm's way.

* * *

In terms of parenting, mothers and fathers have differing opinions on how young black boys should be raised. Having two parents in the home helps ensure a well-balanced child. Notice the difference in relationships between a boy with his mom versus with his dad, a boy with his aunt versus his uncle, or a female teacher versus a male teacher. The nurturing spirit of a woman is so needed for a boy to feel love, to open up, and to be able to express himself. Oftentimes, boys are nurtured to complete dependency on their mothers and can grow up and expect women to take care of them. And why not? That's what they are used to. Yes, black men have it hard out here, but coddling little black boys is not helping them get ready to face the world. What they are being taught is that no matter what you do, mother will be there for you. No matter if you don't want to work, go to school, move out of the house, or do anything with your life, mom will still care for you. Young black boys need a male figure, or their father in the home to let them know they can't depend on a woman to always be there to comfort and take care of them. Things might not be going as planned, but sometimes you gotta hit the pavement get out there and make it happen.

Chapter 8 ‖ Notable Leaders in Our Community

Lebron James

Lebron James is one of the most decorated basketball players and future hall of famers in the NBA right now. He is often regarded as the greatest player of all time, which has resulted in frequent comparisons to Michael Jordan. His accomplishments include three NBA championships, four NBA Most Valuable Player (MVP) awards, three Finals MVP awards, and two Olympic gold medals. He is ranked as one of America's most influential and popular athletes. He has been featured in books, documentaries, and television commercials.

While Lebron James has an impressive basketball resume, what makes him so special to me is his activism. He is an active supporter of non-profit organizations, such as Boys and Girls Clubs of America and the Children's Defense fund. He has his own charity foundation, the Lebron James Family Foundation, that raises money for various causes. He has built the I Promise School, a public elementary school created to help struggling students stay in school. He has been outspoken on and taken stances on many controversial issues including the Trayvon

Martin case, the Michael Brown verdict, and the death of Eric Garner. He has one of the biggest platforms for black people and he is using it to highlight injustice.

During a 17-minute interview with ESPN's Cari Champion, Lebron discussed his family, personal growth, and challenges that come with being black and a public figure.

When discussing Trump he said, "The No. 1 job in America, the appointed person is someone who doesn't understand the people," adding that some of the president's comments are "laughable and scary."

In response, Fox News reporter, Laura Ingraham said, "It's always unwise to seek political advice from someone who gets paid $100 million a year to bounce a ball.". "Keep the political comments to yourself. Shut up and dribble." With all the good things this man has done and been involved with, how is that because he is an athlete he can't have an opinion? Obviously, every American voter has an opinion because that's how they determine who they're going to vote for.

Lebron James did not "shut up and dribble". Instead, he made a three-part documentary series, titled "Shut Up and Dribble", that provides an inside look at the changing role of athletes in today's cultural and political environments. In a time when comments about race still linger, this series shows the influence athletes have and how they should not shut up and dribble.

Nipsey Hussle

There is an unspoken code to living in poverty that goes a little something like this: People want to see you do good, but not too good because then, you are assumed to think you're better than your counterparts. Rapper Nipsey Hussle speaks about this in his song "Don't Take Days Off" when he states:

> How the hell you supposed to know what
> to do when nobody showed you the
> ropes
>
> All they showed you was pistols and dope
>
> Gang flags in the land with no hope
>
> Where every fitted hat mean a different
> hood
>
> Make it out & they still want you in the
> hood
>
> Your own homies don't want you livin'
> good

This hurts me because those last two lines are the reason he is dead now. This man was a former gang member who changed his life around to become a rapper, community activist, and entrepreneur. He worked to empower and employ underprivileged groups through real estate investments, science, and tech learning centers for teens. Yet, with all the good he was doing for his former community, some didn't appreciate it. He was shot in front of the clothing store he owned, where he provided jobs for a lot of young people. While most saw him as an inspiration to make it out the hood and do better for yourself, there were others who disregarded that and saw him as a meal ticket or a sellout. He is added to a list of rappers killed by members of their own community. Senseless murders because of jealousy and hatred.

Nipsey Hussle's death could be attributed to being at the wrong place at the wrong time. Maybe he was killed because he had hope for his community and wanted to show that even though he had made it, he still wanted to come back and show support. This is a perfect example of how living in poverty is a mindset. It is full of do's and don'ts that only those who live in it know about. The way you view outsiders with money and resources is the same way they will view you if you obtain such. You work your whole life to defeat the struggle. Then you make it, only to get taken out by people you struggled with. It's a sad situation, but it happens so often. Growing up in poverty affects you from childhood all the way through adulthood. As a former member of communities like this you want to help but you can't forget how ruthless and violent individuals can be.

People existing in poverty actually feel good about themselves when they can look next door and see somebody going through the same struggle as they are. It's weird but it's comforting, because you don't feel alone. You have a community that doesn't have much, but at least you have each other. I know this feeling because I have lived. You don't need much, just good people around and you can get through the day.

Colin Kaepernick

This former NFL quarterback and activist may not have his pro-football job back, but his presence and influence still resonates off the field. During a pre-season game in 2016, Kaepernick was noticed sitting down during the playing of "The Star-Spangled Banner '', as opposed to the tradition of standing. During a post-game interview, he explained his position stating, "I am not going to stand up to show pride in a flag for a country that oppresses black people and people of color. There are bodies in the street and people getting paid leave and getting away with murder," he said, referencing a series of African American deaths by law enforcement that led to the BLACK LIVES MATTER movement.

Since taking a knee to protest racism and police brutality in 2016, he has been unable to play football. Since then he has founded his own non-profit, the Know Your Rights Camp. He has donated up to $1 million to community groups. Even though he is out of the NFL, support for Kaepernick continues. He asked Nike to pull its limited-edition Betsy Ross flag sneakers, due to racist iconography. The company agreed.

His story is so important because he used his platform to implement change. He placed his beliefs and morals over a financial contract and expressed himself. Sometimes, you have to sacrifice things and stand up for what's right. He will forever be remembered and respected for his stance on racial equality, longer than he ever will for playing football. For this, Colin Kaepernick is a cultural icon.

* * *

74

These successful black men were able to understand the need for change in our country and individual communities, and they chose to do something about it. They were able to use their platform and their voice to address racial inequality, police brutality, and the need for blacks to not tolerate racism. These men changed the narrative of being an athlete, being presumed to stick to sports, and having no say in politics.

About the Author

Emanuel Grimes attended the University of Missouri–St Louis where he majored in Sociology with a minor in Psychology. Upon graduation he felt the need to speak to troubled youth directly and began working at the Oklahoma Juvenile Detention Center. He is no stranger to these institutions having frequented them growing up to visit his own brother. What he noticed there is that the young men craved male attention and that they were really excited to have black male staff. He began to realize the only time some of these guys got to interact with positive male role models is when incarcerated. He was destined to try to change the trajectory of other young men's lives before they ended up in juvenile. By producing *The Black Youth Manual,* he is giving them valuable information and protocol to abide by. Mr. Grimes has two sisters and two brothers, and six nieces and nephews. When he is not around family he spends his time traveling, working out, and volunteering.

www.ingramcontent.com/pod-product-compliance
Lightning Source LLC
Chambersburg PA
CBHW051218250726
48655CB00006B/2485